Original title:
Whispers of Light and Laughter

Copyright © 2025 Swan Charm
All rights reserved.

Author: Kaido Väinamäe
ISBN HARDBACK: 978-9908-1-3520-5
ISBN PAPERBACK: 978-9908-1-3521-2
ISBN EBOOK: 978-9908-1-3522-9

Soft Colors of Joyous Reflection

In the dawn's gentle light,
Soft shades start to play,
Whispering secrets of night,
Chasing shadows away.

With a brush of the breeze,
Colors dance on the skin,
Painting moments with ease,
Where joy can begin.

Golden hues fill the air,
Traces of laughter bright,
Every heart laid bare,
In the warmth of the light.

Clouds drift like thoughts,
In a sky kissed by hope,
With dreams newly sought,
Joy begins to elope.

In the twilight's glow,
Reflections softly wane,
Embracing the flow,
Where peace will remain.

The Laughter that Dances Upon Dreams

In moonlit sighs of delight,
Laughter twirls on the breeze,
Whispers of dreams take flight,
With grace, they aim to please.

Stars wink with a soft cheer,
Playful giggles abound,
Echoes of joy appear,
In the night's gentle sound.

With every joyful leap,
The heart sings a sweet tune,
Awakening from sleep,
Underneath the bright moon.

As dawn comes to embrace,
Laughter lingers still near,
In every cherished space,
Dreams become crystal clear.

With each moment we share,
We dance in gentle bliss,
Finding joy everywhere,
In every stolen kiss.

Luminous Threads of Chuckling Murmurs

Woven through the night air,
Threads of laughter entwine,
Giggles float without care,
In patterns pure and fine.

With each tickle of sound,
Joy cascades like a stream,
Whispers linger around,
Cradling every dream.

In the heart's gentle fold,
Stories start to unfurl,
With warmth, we behold,
Life's vibrant, joyful swirl.

In moments brightly spun,
Mirth echoes in delight,
Granting peace to each one,
As day turns into night.

Through luminous delight,
We cherish each small laugh,
Threads of joy hold us tight,
In the tapestry's path.

Joyful Shadows in the Embrace of Twilight

As twilight softly glows,
Shadows mingle with light,
In this world we compose,
Joy dances through the night.

With every breath we take,
The air hums with delight,
In every step we make,
Shadows twirl in their flight.

Holding hands with the stars,
Heartbeats echo the tune,
Joy whispers from afar,
Beneath the silver moon.

In this serene embrace,
We find comfort and cheer,
Joyful shadows we trace,
Whispering secrets near.

With twilight as our guide,
We embrace the unknown,
In joy, together we bide,
Creating a heartfelt home.

The Bright Chorus of Smiles Alight

In the garden where laughter plays,
Children dance through golden rays.
Every smile a sunlit spark,
Echoes in the joy-filled park.

Whispers of happiness take flight,
Bubbles burst in pure delight.
Moments weave a tapestry,
Threads of love, wild and free.

Sparkling Giggles in the Quiet Glade

Amidst the trees where shadows creep,
Tiny giggles softly leap.
Nature listens to their sound,
Magic in the laughter found.

Leaves sway gently with the breeze,
Dance along with carefree ease.
In this realm of light and glee,
Hearts unite in harmony.

Lumi and Laughter in Twilight Meadows

In twilight's embrace, the stars emerge,
Lumi prances, hearts converge.
Laughter rings through open fields,
Joyful moments, love it yields.

Soft hues paint the fading light,
Whispers weave through warmest night.
As dreams blossom in gentle flow,
Magic starts to freely grow.

Cradled by the Glow of Joyful Moments

In the glow of twilight's peace,
Time stands still, all troubles cease.
Cradled in warmth, hearts entwine,
Capturing moments, pure and divine.

With every laugh, the fire grows,
Brightening paths as soft wind blows.
Memories linger like a song,
Carried where we all belong.

Radiance in Silken Traces

In the morning's gentle hue,
Sunlight dances, soft and new.
Whispers weave through blooming flowers,
Time unfolds in golden hours.

Silken threads of dreams we share,
Brush of joy hangs in the air.
Each moment kissed by fleeting grace,
Together, we find our place.

Laughter lingers on the breeze,
Filling hearts with tranquil ease.
The world reflects our vibrant glow,
In unity, our love will grow.

Stars descend as dusk appears,
Guard our hopes, embrace our fears.
In the night, our hearts ignite,
Guiding us with purest light.

So let us walk in silken threads,
Woven dreams and words unsaid.
Radiance blooms in every space,
Together, we find our grace.

Posies of Cheerful Echoes

Bright petals dance on gentle winds,
In laughter, every heart rescinds.
Together we weave a vibrant song,
In this place, we all belong.

Each voice a note in joyful tune,
Underneath the glowing moon.
Moments shared like sunlit beams,
Traces left in fleeting dreams.

Colors splashed on canvas wide,
In nature's arms, we find our guide.
Posies bloom with every smile,
Joy abounds, let's linger awhile.

Life's echoes spread like morning light,
Awakening the heart's delight.
In the garden, laughter grows,
Each seed planted softly glows.

Together in this cheerful dance,
We grasp at love with every chance.
In dreams, our hearts forever soar,
In posies bright, we ask for more.

The Flicker of Hopeful Laughter

In shadows deep where darkness sings,
Hope arises on gentle wings.
A flicker bright, like stars in night,
Guides our hearts to endless light.

With laughter soft as summer rain,
We find solace, ease our pain.
Together we rise with dreams anew,
In moments shared, our spirits grew.

Hopeful echoes bounce on air,
Filling hearts with vibrant care.
In every smile, a story blooms,
Chasing away the deepest glooms.

The flicker glows with radiant warmth,
A gentle call, a steady charm.
In unity, our dreams ignite,
With laughter, we embrace the night.

So let our voices blend as one,
In joy and hope, we've just begun.
In every heartbeat, laughter flows,
Together—always, hope bestows.

Carnival of Lights and Memories

Underneath the festive skies,
Dancing flames in radiant cries.
The carnival bursts with colors bright,
Shadows fade in the trembling light.

Memories twirl like ribbons spun,
In every laugh, in every run.
Joyful whispers fill the air,
Celebrating moments rare.

Balloons afloat in wild delight,
Carry dreams into the night.
Each spark a tale of love retold,
In every heart, a treasure gold.

The music swells, the laughter roars,
Every face, a canvas pours.
In the magic, we find our way,
Together here, come what may.

Lights flicker like our passions soar,
In this carnival, we explore.
Memories gathered, bright and clear,
In laughter's arms, we hold them dear.

Hues of Merriment and Hope

In the dawn, colors break free,
Whispers of laughter dance on the breeze.
Sunlight pours like liquid gold,
Stories of joy, softly told.

Rainbows arch across the skies,
Each hue a promise, a sweet surprise.
Painted dreams in every heart,
In this canvas, we share a part.

Petals flutter, bright and bold,
In gardens where secrets unfold.
Hope blooms like flowers in spring,
In this beauty, our spirits sing.

Bubbles rise with gleeful cheer,
Floating high with nothing to fear.
Moments twinkle under the sun,
In hues of joy, we weave as one.

As shadows lengthen, colors blend,
Such simple pleasures, we defend.
In each stroke, life finds its thread,
A tapestry of love widespread.

The Sway of Graceful Grins

In the meadow, laughter weaves,
Softly swaying like the leaves.
Children play with boundless glee,
Their smiles are pure, wild, and free.

Under the arch of a sunny hue,
Faces spark like the morning dew.
Graceful steps, a joyful dance,
Each movement alive with romance.

A gentle breeze carries the sound,
Of giggles and cheer all around.
The world spins with delight and care,
In the sway of joy, love fills the air.

Bright eyes twinkle, spirits soar,
Inviting all to join the lore.
With every grin, hearts intertwine,
In this moment, we dare to shine.

As the day fades into dreams,
The laughter lingers, a soft gleam.
In every jest, we find a friend,
Where the sway of smiles will never end.

Shimmering Trails of Amusement

Starlight glimmers on the stream,
Reflecting wonders that make us dream.
Footsteps light upon the ground,
In this magic, joy is found.

Puppets dance in the moonlit glow,
Chasing shadows, to and fro.
Each giggle echoes through the night,
Painting darkness with pure delight.

Laughter rides upon the wind,
A symphony where dreams rescind.
Whispers tangle, spirits rise,
In the play, our spirit flies.

Tickling secrets held so tight,
Bring forth smiles, banish fright.
With each jest, we weave our tale,
On shimmering trails where we prevail.

As dawn approaches, colors blend,
The echoes fade, but heart can mend.
In every chuckle, love we find,
A trail of amusement left behind.

Whimsical Shadows of Elation

In the twilight, shadows bloom,
Whimsical forms dispel the gloom.
Dancing light on faces bright,
Feasting on laughter, a pure delight.

The moon raises a playful brow,
As giggles float, enchanting vow.
Whispers twine in a gentle chase,
In this moment, we find our place.

Masked figures prance and twirl,
In shimmering dreams, our hearts unfurl.
Each chuckle weaves a tender bond,
Elation's echoes, endless and beyond.

Under stars, joy is sewn,
In tight-knit circles, seeds are grown.
With every flicker, spirits soar,
In the shadows, we explore.

As dawn breaks, colors ignite,
The shadows bow to morning light.
Yet in our hearts, the fire stays,
Whimsical elation forever plays.

Whispering Colors of Happiness

In gardens where the laughter blooms,
The petals dance with joy and light.
Each shade a song, a sweet perfume,
A brush of love that feels so right.

The sun spills gold on morning dew,
As whispers weave through trees so tall.
In every hue, the heart finds new,
The vibrant threads that bind us all.

Clouds of pink blend with the blue,
A canvas painted fresh each day.
With every smile, life feels brand new,
In colors bright, we'll find our way.

Together we create the art,
In laughter shared, our dreams take flight.
With every beat, we play our part,
In the embrace of pure delight.

So let us chase the hues that gleam,
And capture joy in every glance.
In fields of hope, we dare to dream,
In whispered colors, we will dance.

Smiles Unfurled in the Morning Breeze

In dawn's soft glow, the world awakes,
With gentle whispers of the day.
Each smile a step that joy partakes,
As nature sings in bright array.

The breeze carries laughter through the trees,
A chorus sweet that lifts our hearts.
With every breath, we feel the ease,
As sunlight warms, and shadows part.

Beneath the sky, so vast and clear,
We greet the morn with open arms.
The warmth invites, dissolves all fear,
With every smile, a world transforms.

Among the flowers, joy takes flight,
As petals dance in summer's light.
Together, let us chase the bright,
With hearts entwined, in pure delight.

So raise your gaze to azure skies,
And let the laughter fill the air.
In every smile that freely flies,
We find a magic, bold and rare.

Radiance Wrapped in Playful Echoes

The echoes ring where laughter roams,
In every corner, joy resounds.
With playful hearts, we weave our homes,
In radiant light, our love abounds.

Through fields of dreams, we skip and sway,
In vibrant hues, our spirits soar.
The playful echoes guide our way,
A melody we can't ignore.

Each moment shared, a golden thread,
That binds us close in unity.
With every word, the worries shed,
We bloom together, wild and free.

In candlelight, our laughter glows,
Reflecting joy in every face.
The warmth of friendship softly flows,
In playful echoes, we find grace.

So let the world hear our delight,
As joy reverberates through time.
Wrapped in radiance, we take flight,
In echoes sweet, our hearts align.

The Joy that Twinkles in the Twilight

As twilight paints the sky with dreams,
The stars awake to dance above.
In whispered secrets, night redeems,
A canvas strewn with peace and love.

With gentle glow, the moonlight spills,
A silver trail on paths we roam.
In every heart, the quiet thrills,
As night unfolds, we find our home.

The world grows still, the magic sings,
In silhouettes, the stories play.
With every breath, our spirit clings,
To twilight's charm that guides our way.

Beneath the stars, we make a vow,
To cherish moments crisp and clear.
In joyful twinkles, here and now,
We weave our dreams without a fear.

So let the night embrace our bliss,
As laughter twinkles in the dark.
In every glance, a fleeting kiss,
The joy of twilight leaves its mark.

Echoes of Radiant Joy

In the meadow where dreams play,
Laughter dances on the breeze,
Colors bloom in bright array,
Time seems to pause with ease.

Whispered tales of warmth unfold,
Beneath the vast, cerulean sky,
Memories wrapped in threads of gold,
Here, every heart learns to fly.

Joyful voices linger near,
Singing praises to the light,
Each echo, soft and clear,
Guides us through the endless night.

As shadows blend with the dawn,
Hope awakens, fresh and bright,
In every soul, a spark is drawn,
Together, we ignite the night.

Here, where radiant joy lives,
And all the world feels like home,
The heart's pure song forever gives,
A place where love is free to roam.

Flickers of Delightful Secrets

In the dusk, where whispers hide,
Secrets linger, soft and sweet,
Flickers dance by fire's side,
Creating magic in the heat.

Silent smiles and knowing glances,
Underneath the twinkling stars,
Life becomes a series of chances,
As night unveils its hidden jars.

Each flicker tells a story true,
Of laughter shared and dreams that soar,
Moments rare, just me and you,
Bound together, forevermore.

The gentle hush of evening's grace,
Wraps around our quiet sighs,
In this sacred, cherished space,
Delightful secrets weave the skies.

As shadows deepen, hearts ignite,
Embracing every tender spark,
In flickers of delightful light,
We dance until the morning dark.

Chasing Sunbeams and Smiles

Through fields of gold, we roam free,
Chasing sunbeams, laughing bright,
With every step, pure glee we see,
As hearts gleam in the gentle light.

Hand in hand, we weave our dreams,
Embracing warmth that summer brings,
Laughter flows like sparkling streams,
Joy resides in simple things.

With each smile, the world ignites,
Colors burst in vibrant sway,
In every heart, a love that lights,
Guiding us throughout the day.

We run where wildflowers bloom,
Lost in wonders, time stands still,
In every corner, life finds room,
Chasing sunbeams, hearts fulfilled.

And when the evening sun descends,
With soft kisses from the sky,
In cherished moments, love transcends,
Transforming every tear to sigh.

Songs of Glistening Mirth

In the twilight, laughter rings,
Songs of mirth take flight and soar,
With every note, the heartstrings sing,
Melodies echo evermore.

Whispers of joy dance in the air,
As moonlight weaves through the trees,
Glistening moments, precious and rare,
Filling souls with gentle ease.

The stars respond with twinkling light,
Illuminating cheerful hearts,
Drawing us close, into the night,
Where every song of love imparts.

With each chord, we find our way,
Through laughter's embrace, we ignite,
In songs of glistening, vibrant play,
We find the warmth of pure delight.

Together, we spin tales of old,
Through each melody, dreams set free,
In timeless rhythms, love is told,
Finding bliss in harmony.

Heartstrings Twirling in the Glimmering Mist

In the mist where dreams reside,
Heartstrings dance, they swell with pride.
Whispers soft, like morning light,
Guiding souls through endless night.

Each note plays a melody sweet,
In this realm where echoes meet.
Colors weave, a tapestry bright,
Lifting spirits to new height.

Through the fog, a path unfolds,
Stories waiting to be told.
Joy and sorrow intertwined,
In this world, our hearts aligned.

The Brightness of Souls in Unison

In the glow of shared delight,
Souls unite, igniting light.
Horizons blend in vibrant hue,
Together we are ever new.

Voices rise, a gentle choir,
Touching hearts, our dreams aspire.
With every laugh, a spark ignites,
Creating warmth on chilly nights.

In the dance of life, we sway,
Collective joy, our hearts convey.
Through every trial, hand in hand,
In unison, we boldly stand.

Luminous Cadences of Bliss

Softly hums the wind's embrace,
Luminous whispers time and space.
Melodies swirl like autumn's breeze,
Filling hearts with gentle ease.

Each cadence tells a story true,
Of love awaiting me and you.
With every beat, the cosmos sings,
Embracing all the joy it brings.

In the rhythm of the stars,
We find our hopes, we trace our scars.
A symphony of dreams unfurled,
In these rhythms, we find our world.

Laughter's Embrace in the Morning Glow

In the morning light so bright,
Laughter dances, pure delight.
Joyful echoes fill the air,
Binding hearts in a tender care.

Every chuckle, a sweet refrain,
Chasing shadows, easing pain.
With each smile, the world awakes,
In this warmth, the spirit shakes.

Beneath the sky's embracing blue,
Laughter blossoms, bold and true.
In this moment, we belong,
In laughter's dance, forever strong.

Fables of Kindness and Radiance

In a world of shadows, a light will gleam,
Whispers of kindness, like a gentle dream.
Hands that reach out, hearts that embrace,
Each act of goodness, a warm, bright trace.

Stories of courage, in silence they flow,
Lessons of love, they gently bestow.
A simple smile, a friendly gesture,
Fables of kindness, our greatest treasure.

The Glow of Happy Hearts and Whimsy

Beneath the starlight, laughter takes flight,
Happy hearts gather, painting the night.
With every chuckle, the shadows retreat,
Whimsy and joy dance, so light on their feet.

In the glow of laughter, we find our way,
Brightening the moments of each passing day.
Together we shine, our spirits entwined,
In the warmth of friendship, true magic we find.

Dancing in the Glow of Wonder

In the twilight hour, dreams softly blend,
Dancing in wonder, where the skies mend.
Stars above twinkle, like eyes full of glee,
A celestial ballet, wild and carefree.

With every heartbeat, the magic unfolds,
Stories of old, in the night gently told.
We sway with the moonlight, as shadows all play,
In the glow of wonder, we drift and we sway.

Gentle Breezes and Hushed Chuckles

Gentle breezes whisper through the trees,
Carrying laughter, soft as the leaves.
In the hush of the night, sweet secrets reside,
With each gentle chuckle, our hearts open wide.

Under moonlit skies, we share our delight,
Every soft sigh, an echo of light.
Together in stillness, we cherish the sound,
Of gentle breezes and joy that we've found.

Flickers of Delight Amongst the Shadows

In the hush of twilight, they glow,
Soft whispers of joy, a gentle show.
Shadows dance lightly, a fleeting game,
In each secret flicker, there lies a flame.

Moonbeams sprinkle silver on trees,
Inviting the night with a playful breeze.
Each laugh from the darkness, a spark alights,
Bringing forth warmth on cool, starry nights.

Dreams intertwine with the swaying air,
Laughter that lingers, a soft, tender care.
Moments of bliss in the dimming light,
Flickers of hope that chase away fright.

A serenade echoes beneath the stars,
Joyful refrains of life's open bars.
In every shadow, a story concealed,
Flickers of delight, softly revealed.

Embrace each sparkle that travels the night,
In shadows, we find our hearts take flight.
Through flickering joy, we find a way,
To dance with the dusk, to live, to play.

Swaying with Radiant Cheer and Whimsy

Beneath the sun's smile, we sway and twirl,
A dance of delight in a colorful whirl.
Each petal that flutters, a joyous tune,
Spinning with laughter, beneath the moon.

Whimsy takes hold in each golden ray,
Brightening hearts in a playful display.
Giggles erupt from the flowers that bloom,
Casting away shadows, dispelling the gloom.

With every breeze, we leap and glide,
Radiant cheer is our faithful guide.
In the garden of dreams, we frolic and play,
Embracing the magic of each fleeting day.

Swaying together, we find our beat,
Moments of bliss, oh, so sweet.
We gather the laughter like petals in hand,
Creating a symphony across the land.

A tapestry woven with threads of delight,
In the warmth of the day, we find our light.
With whimsy as our compass, we roam,
Creating our joy, our hearts, our home.

A Symphony of Glimmering Glee

In corners of dreams, a melody plays,
Notes of laughter dance through the haze.
With every heartbeat, the joy unfolds,
In whispers of light, a story told.

Glimmers arise, like stars in the night,
Each spark ignites the soul's pure delight.
A symphony woven of moments so bright,
Reminds us of love, of hope, and of flight.

With twinkling harmonies, we glide along,
In a waltz of bliss, we find where we belong.
Each note a heartbeat, a radiant spark,
Filling the silence that once held the dark.

As violins sing of the joy intertwined,
With laughter as lyrics, our spirits aligned.
A symphony crafted in the heart's domain,
Where glimmering glee dances unchained.

Through shifting crescendos, we soar and dive,
In the embrace of the music, we come alive.
With every refrain, we joyously vow,
To cherish the glee that whispers, here and now.

Sighs of Sunshine and Breezy Chuckles

Warm rays peek through the leaves,
Laughter dances in the air.
Nature hums a gentle tune,
Embracing joys beyond compare.

Whispers of the golden morn,
Flutter softly on the breeze.
Each moment feels like a gift,
Bringing hearts to feel at ease.

Smiles bloom like wildflowers,
In fields where sunlight spills.
Every chuckle lifts the soul,
As happiness fulfills.

Twirling shadows, playful light,
Weaving dreams in sunny threads.
Sighs of bliss, a sweet embrace,
Where laughter gently spreads.

Luminous Heartstrings and Soft Laughter

Stars twinkle in the night sky,
Heartstrings hum a tender song.
Laughter echoes through the dark,
A melody where we belong.

Whispers of joy fill the air,
In every corner, every turn.
Soft laughter lights the shadows,
And all our worries burn.

Glow of dreams in peaceful nights,
Wraps us in a warm cocoon.
With heartstrings tied together,
We sway beneath the silver moon.

In this quiet, sacred space,
Life's magic truly starts.
Luminous whispers fill the night,
Binding together our hearts.

Glistening Pathways of Cheer

Amidst the trees, the sunlight gleams,
Pathways carved with joy awake.
Every turn brings happy dreams,
As laughter sways in every shake.

Glistening leaves, bright drops of dew,
Kiss the earth with gentle mirth.
Cheerful steps make the journey light,
Bringing joy to every birth.

Voices echo soft and sweet,
As we wander, hand in hand.
Nature sings where hearts can meet,
In this enchanted, loving land.

The world shines bright with vibrant hues,
In every smile, a spark ignites.
Glistening pathways filled with cheer,
Guiding us through love's delights.

The Harmony of Light and Amusement

Light pours down in golden streams,
Capturing moments pure and bright.
Amusement dances in our eyes,
As shadows play in warm daylight.

Joy unfolds in every laugh,
A symphony of sheer delight.
Harmony sways in the breeze,
Wrapping us in soft twilight.

Lively tunes twist through the air,
Echoing the rhythms of cheer.
Days unfold like sweetened dreams,
Each laughter captures what is dear.

Together we create a world,
Where light and fun forever blend.
In harmony, our spirits rise,
A joyful melody we send.

Murmurs of Sunshine and Bliss

Golden rays softly weave,
Through trees that gently dance,
Whispers of the morning light,
A sweet and hopeful glance.

Birds sing songs of pure delight,
In the warmth of bright blue skies,
Nature's laughter fills the air,
As every heart begins to rise.

Petals flutter in the breeze,
Colors burst in fragrant bloom,
Every moment softly speaks,
In the garden's softened room.

With each step, our spirits soar,
Chasing dreams on sunlit trails,
Together in this blissful state,
Our laughter dances, never fails.

Embrace the light, let shadows fade,
In cocoon of joy, we bask,
Murmurs of the sun's sweet grace,
In our hearts, a treasured task.

Glimmers of Playful Serenity

In fields where daisies sway,
Children's laughter fills the air,
Sunshine sparkles on the grass,
A moment free from every care.

Clouds drift lazily above,
Like whispers soft and slight,
As giggles chase the gentle breeze,
The world feels warm and bright.

In every heart, a tune awakens,
A melody of playful bliss,
With every step, a joy we find,
In simple moments like this.

Bubbles dance on summer's breath,
Chasing rainbows in the sun,
Each glimmer shown, a fleeting gift,
This playful day, we've just begun.

So let the laughter soar and rise,
In glimmers of sweet, pure glee,
A symphony of innocence,
In nature's happy jubilee.

The Dance of Gleaming Giggles

Round and round, the children twirl,
In a circle bright and free,
Their giggles echo through the air,
A joyful, sweet decree.

With every step, the world ignites,
A dance beyond compare,
As bubbles float to greet the sun,
In the warm and tender air.

Little feet on soft green grass,
Like starlings taking flight,
They leap and bound with purest joy,
Underneath the blue, bright light.

Each smile shares a glimmering thought,
Of dreams that bloom and grow,
In this dance of gleaming giggles,
Our hearts begin to glow.

Let this moment last forever,
In laughter's sweet embrace,
The dance of life, so full of love,
In every shining face.

Reflections in a Joyful Glow

In quiet moments, peace unfolds,
As sunsets paint the sky,
Golden hues invite the night,
With twinkling stars gone shy.

Each glimmer glances off the lake,
Where whispers softly pass,
A dance of light upon the waves,
In nature's soothing glass.

The world reflects a gentle grace,
In every fleeting glow,
As laughter ripples through our thoughts,
Like sunlight on the snow.

With every heartbeat, joy resounds,
The present's sweet embrace,
Reflections of a treasured life,
In time's enchanting space.

So gather 'round the fire's warmth,
Share stories of delight,
In the glow of joyful moments,
We find our hearts take flight.

Illuminated Dreams and Joyful Hearts

In the twilight's gentle glow,
Whispers of magic flow,
Hearts dance with pure delight,
Chasing stars into the night.

Echoes of laughter ring,
As the night birds softly sing,
Dreams woven through the air,
With a promise, light and fair.

Moonlight kisses weary eyes,
As the world in slumber lies,
In dreams, we find our spark,
Guided gently through the dark.

Joyous hearts, they intertwine,
In a rhythm, sweet and fine,
Underneath the silver beams,
Lost in our illuminated dreams.

As dawn breaks with hues of gold,
New stories waiting to be told,
With each breath, a brand new chance,
To weave life's enchanting dance.

Jests Beneath the Canvas of Sky

Beneath the vast and endless blue,
Where laughter paints the world anew,
Jests and japes in playful flight,
Chasing clouds, pure and light.

A canvas stretched from sea to land,
With colors bright, a brush in hand,
Imagination takes its course,
Where whimsy reigns, a vibrant force.

Children's laughter fills the air,
Glimmering eyes, without a care,
Every pair of skimming feet,
Falls in time with primal beat.

An artist's dream, a poet's muse,
In playful thoughts, we often lose,
Underneath the summer's sun,
Life unfurls, a game unrun.

As twilight falls, the jesters fade,
But in our hearts, the joy is laid,
Stories linger, memories fly,
Forever jests beneath the sky.

The Flicker of Hopeful Grins

In shadows deep, a light appears,
Bringing warmth to untold fears,
A flicker caught in fleeting time,
Hope dances softly, pure and prime.

Each smile a beacon, bright and clear,
Chasing away the doubt and fear,
In silent moments, truth unfurls,
Through hopeful grins, our spirit twirls.

Gathered close, we share our dreams,
In the quiet, laughter beams,
Supporting one another's rise,
Together, we touch the skies.

A spark ignites within the soul,
Binding hearts to make us whole,
Through trials faced, we find our place,
In every tear, a smile's trace.

So let us treasure every grin,
For in each pulse, we truly win,
With flickers bright and spirits free,
Hopeful grins, our legacy.

Sunkissed Tales of Merriment

In golden light, the laughter flows,
Where merry hearts and friendship grows,
Sunkissed days, a joyful cheer,
As stories shared draw us near.

With each sunset, hues align,
Memories etched, a sweet design,
Echoes of joy in gentle play,
As twilight hugs the close of day.

Through fields of dreams, we skip and run,
Bathed in warmth, 'neath the sun,
With every step, our spirits soar,
While the waves crash on the shore.

Laughter dances on the breeze,
Bringing forth life's simple pleas,
Tales of hope and love retold,
A treasure chest of joy untold.

So here's to days of merriment,
In every moment, pure content,
With sunkissed skins and beating hearts,
Life's tale of joy, where love imparts.

Gleams of Humor Beneath Starlit Canopies

Under the stars where laughter sways,
Jokes are woven in the night's soft haze.
Twinkling lights and friendly cheer,
Joyful voices fill the atmosphere.

Moonbeams dance on whispers bright,
Witty tales take joyful flight.
In shadows where the spirits play,
Humor glimmers, lighting our way.

Chasing dreams through the cosmic stream,
Each chuckle adds to laughter's beam.
With every giggle, worries cease,
In this starlit realm, we find our peace.

Under the canopy, we share our dreams,
In vibrant hues and playful schemes.
The night wears joy like a velvet crown,
As we spin tales and joyfully clown.

So let us revel in this sacred space,
Where humor finds a warm embrace.
Gleams of laughter guide us home,
Beneath the sky where spirits roam.

Sunkissed Whispers of Cheerful Spirits

Morning sun brings smiles anew,
Cheerful spirits dance in view.
Breezes carry laughter free,
Sunkissed whispers, harmony.

In gardens where the flowers bloom,
Joyful hearts dispel all gloom.
With every petal kissed by light,
Happiness takes eager flight.

Children's laughter fills the air,
In every sound, love is laid bare.
Through the trees, sweet melodies sing,
Under the sky, our spirits spring.

Moments cherished, forever bright,
With sunlit days, we feel the light.
Memories painted in joyful hues,
Sunkissed whispers, we embrace the views.

So let us gather, hand in hand,
In this sunlit, joyful land.
With cheerful spirits, we shall stay,
Embracing light, come what may.

The Lightness of Being with Sparkling Joy

In moments small where laughter thrives,
Joyfulness dances, and spirit dives.
The heart flutters, a feather's grace,
In lightness found, we find our place.

Each giggle shared, a treasure true,
With sparkling joy, the world feels new.
Bright eyes twinkle in playful glee,
As life unfolds, we feel set free.

Wonders abound in every day,
With lightness in our hearts, we play.
A gentle breeze, a radiant smile,
In joyful moments, we bask a while.

Floating on dreams, like clouds above,
With arms wide open, we share our love.
In bonds unspoken, our spirits soar,
With sparkling joy, who could ask for more?

So let us dance through fields of gold,
In the lightness of being, together we hold.
With every laugh, we weave our fate,
In joyful harmony, we celebrate.

Echoes of Serenity and Playful Revelry

In quiet corners, peace does bloom,
Echoes of laughter dispel the gloom.
Moments cherished in simple play,
Within our hearts, a gentle sway.

Under the trees where shadows blend,
Serenity joins with laughter's end.
Whimsical thoughts take flight on high,
As joy fills the air, spirits fly.

Ripples dance on a tranquil sea,
Where carefree whispers roam wild and free.
In every heartbeat, a joyful sound,
Echoes of revelry all around.

In the tapestry of night's embrace,
We weave our dreams in a sacred space.
With laughter's song, our souls unite,
Echoes of joy take dazzling flight.

So let us gather, hand in hand,
In the gentle rhythm that life has planned.
With serenity's grace and laughter's swell,
We find our haven, our shared carousel.

Glimmers of Mischief Underneath the Stars

In the hush of night, whispers rise,
Little pranks dance 'neath starlit skies.
Glows of laughter, secrets shared,
A sprinkle of dreams in mischief bared.

The moonlight plays on shadows' games,
Chasing echoes, calling names.
With winks and grins, they convene,
In a world of wonder, bright and keen.

Around the fire, stories unfold,
Adventures painted bright and bold.
Crickets sing, the night ignites,
In glimmers of mischief, hearts take flight.

Stars twinkle down, a mischievous crew,
With every glance, new ideas brew.
In the presence of magic, all fears flee,
For mischief blooms in jubilee.

As dawn approaches, the giggles soar,
With memories made, they crave even more.
In the morning light, they fade away,
Leaving behind the joy of play.

Murmurs in the Golden Glow

In the soft light of the setting sun,
Whispers of joy, where laughter's spun.
Golden rays dance, touching the earth,
Each moment shines with untold worth.

Gentle breezes carry sweet calls,
Echoes of life in secret halls.
Dreams awaken, softly aglow,
In the warmth of light, their stories flow.

Meadows sway, the flowers nod,
Nature's symphony, a gentle prod.
In the hush of dusk, hearts align,
United by whispers, so divine.

As shadows stretch, the world takes pause,
Reflecting on beauty, without flaws.
In every murmur, magic sings,
In the golden glow, joy it brings.

With every breath, hope intertwines,
As the sun dips low and softly shines.
Secrets linger in the twilight's embrace,
In every murmur, we find our place.

Chasing Shadows with Laughter

As daylight wanes, shadows start to play,
They stretch and yawn at the end of the day.
With each footstep, the giggles grow,
In chase of shadows, laughter flows.

Through winding paths, they dart and weave,
In the golden hour, they truly believe.
With spins and twirls, they dance with glee,
Chasing whispers of what could be.

The world a stage, under twilight's hue,
Every shadow tells a story anew.
In vibrant hues of orange and gold,
Laughter echoes, adventures unfold.

In the twilight hour, friendship ignites,
As shadows meld in the softening lights.
Together they soar, hearts in full sway,
Chasing shadows that lead the way.

With every giggle, the night grows bright,
In the chase of dreams, they find their light.
In whispers of joy, they play and tease,
In laughter's embrace, they find sweet ease.

Secrets Carried on Gentle Rays

In the dawn's blush, whispers arise,
Secrets held close, under soft skies.
Radiant beams stretch, brushing the land,
Carrying promises, gentle and grand.

In the tender light, hopes softly gleam,
As day unfurls, dreams take wing to dream.
A symphony hums on the winds of chance,
In the dance of life, they gently prance.

Golden rays weave through the trees,
Carrying tales on a playful breeze.
Every leaf glimmers with stories old,
In the light, all mysteries are told.

As shadows recede, truths come alive,
In the warmth of day, the spirits thrive.
Underneath the sun, their dreams arise,
Caught in the magic that softly lies.

With each passing moment, hopes will sway,
In the brilliance of light, they gently play.
Secrets carried on gentle rays,
Unfolding the beauty of all our days.

Playful Secrets in the Dawn's Embrace

In the hush of dawn's first light,
Whispers dance, shadows take flight.
Softly giggles the world awake,
Secrets in the breeze we make.

Golden hues touch every leaf,
Promises linger, sweet and brief.
Morning laughter fills the air,
Joy unchained, without a care.

Footprints mark the dewy grass,
Moments fleeting, yet they last.
Chasing dreams where hopes align,
Hearts entwined in warm decline.

Sunrise spills like honeyed gold,
Stories whispered, yet untold.
In this light, we are so free,
Secrets blend in harmony.

As the day begins to wake,
Nature sings for joy's own sake.
In the dawn's embrace we find,
Playful secrets intertwined.

Breezes Boasting of Joyful Secrets

Breezes stir the summer air,
Laughter rings from everywhere.
Secrets carried on the wind,
Joyful tales, where dreams begin.

Skies are blue, the sun aglow,
Whispers dance, and breezes flow.
Children play near blooming flowers,
Each moment rich with vibrant hours.

In the laughter lies the sound,
Of joyful secrets all around.
Nature's symphony we share,
In every breath, love is declared.

Summer shades and twilight gleams,
Fulfill our hopes, support our dreams.
With each gust, our spirits soar,
In breezes boasting, we explore.

Underneath the starlit sky,
We find our place, we learn to fly.
With open hearts and hands to greet,
Joyful secrets bittersweet.

Radiant Echoes of Childhood Joy

In the echoes of laughter bright,
Childhood dances in pure delight.
Moments cherished, never fade,
Memories wrapped in a sweet cascade.

Glorious days beneath the sun,
Chasing tales, oh how we run.
With wild dreams, we touch the sky,
Radiant echoes, never shy.

Every swing and every slide,
Brings a world that we confide.
Moments blend like colors new,
In a canvas painted blue.

Nature's playground calls our name,
In the dusk, our hearts aflame.
With every giggle, every cheer,
Childhood joy remains so near.

As twilight whispers soft and low,
We hold on tight to what we know.
In radiant echoes, dreams reside,
Childhood's joy, our steadfast guide.

Dancing Shadows and Delightful Uncertainties

Underneath the crescent moon,
Shadows sway, a haunting tune.
In the night, we start to roam,
Finding paths that feel like home.

Delightful doubts whisper low,
Where the wild uncertainties flow.
Taking steps with hearts agleam,
Dancing shadows weave a dream.

With every turn, a tale unfolds,
Mysteries wrapped in twilight's folds.
Caught between the push and pull,
Where love is fierce and life is full.

Misty thoughts drift like the air,
Embracing all, with gentle care.
In the stillness, thoughts combine,
Together in this dance we twine.

As dawn approaches, light will break,
All our dreams begin to wake.
In dancing shadows, we arise,
Delightful truths beneath the skies.

Echoes of Radiant Joy

In fields where laughter sways,
The notes of joy hum bright and clear,
Children's whispers fill the days,
A melody we hold so dear.

Each heartstrings strum a playful tune,
While daisies nod in gentle breeze,
Underneath the warm, soft moon,
Time pauses as the soul finds ease.

With every beat, the spirit flies,
Like butterflies in summer's glow,
The world transforms with blissful sighs,
Where every glance sparks joy to flow.

In echoes, memories intertwine,
Fleeting moments captured bright,
In laughter's arms, we choose to shine,
Creating dreams in pure delight.

So let's embrace this vibrant light,
And dance like flowers in full bloom,
Our souls igniting, taking flight,
In echoes of joy, we find room.

Flickers of Forgotten Smiles

In shadows where the echoes fade,
A timid light begins to gleam,
With whispers held, memories laid,
Flickers of joy weave through a dream.

The world moves on, but hearts can cling,
To laughter lost in time's embrace,
A gentle touch, a warm heart's ring,
Awakens smiles from silent space.

Beneath the weight of daily grind,
These gems of joy, though rare, still shine,
In every hug, a love defined,
A timeless bond, so sweet, divine.

Let not the fleeting moments pass,
For in each laugh, a story spins,
A tapestry that we amass,
Reminders of where joy begins.

So hold these flickers close and tight,
Let them ignite the night's soft hue,
In every heart, the spark ignites,
Forgotten smiles, forever new.

Laughter in the Veil of Dawn

As sun peeks through the weeping trees,
The morning breaks, a gentle sigh,
With laughter dancing on the breeze,
The day awakens, birds reply.

In softest hues, the light unfolds,
Embracing whispers, sweet and mild,
A canvas painted, purest golds,
Where every shadow is beguiled.

With every beam, a giggle glows,
Each joyous note a heart's delight,
In soft embrace, the spirit grows,
The veil of dawn, a wondrous sight.

As time unfurls its tender hand,
In every moment, joy's refrain,
Let's wander through this vibrant land,
With laughter echoing like a train.

So rise with me, let worries cease,
In every dawn, find love's own song,
As laughter weaves a thread of peace,
In morning light, we all belong.

The Dance of Sunbeams and Giggles

In meadows bright where children play,
The sunbeams dance on dewy grass,
With giggles ringing through the day,
Moments fleeting, yet they amass.

Each twirl ignites the air with cheer,
As petals sway with joyous grace,
In every smile, our hearts draw near,
An endless rhythm, a warm embrace.

The world can pause, an instant caught,
In sparks of laughter ever true,
With every step, a lesson taught,
In simple joys, we find our cue.

So let's rejoice in this sweet spree,
With sun-kissed dreams that fill the skies,
Together, in pure harmony,
We dance through life with open eyes.

In every giggle, a story spins,
Each sunbeam whispers tales anew,
The dance of life, where joy begins,
With sunbeams bright, we'll chase what's true.

A Tapestry Woven with Light and Laughter

Threads of gold weave through the day,
Laughter dances, bright and gay.
Sunbeams flicker, shadows flee,
Joy wraps us in its warm decree.

Moments gathered, stitched in time,
Every heartbeat, a gentle rhyme.
Colors blend in vibrant hues,
The tapestry old yet forever new.

In the silence, whispers find,
The echo of a loving mind.
Memories stitched with care and grace,
A tapestry of every face.

Twinkling stars at dusk appear,
Laughter echoes, sweet and clear.
Weaving dreams that softly glide,
In this fabric, we abide.

A dance of light upon our soul,
Together, we become the whole.
In laughter's glow, we feel so right,
A tapestry woven with pure light.

The Gleeful Echo of Radiant Hearts

In the morning's golden glow,
Radiance spills, warm and slow.
Echoed giggles fill the air,
A joyful tune beyond compare.

Hearts are dancing, spirits soar,
In this moment, we explore.
Like flowers blooming, bright and free,
We celebrate our unity.

With every beat, our laughter sings,
Joyful whispers on gentle wings.
A symphony of love and cheer,
In this echo, we hold dear.

Through winding paths, hand in hand,
Together we make our stand.
In radiant light, we find our way,
Gleeful echoes guide our stay.

As stars align in evening's grace,
Each shining heart finds its place.
In this union, brightly spun,
The gleeful echo of hearts as one.

Joyful Starlight and Playful Delights

Underneath the starlit sky,
Delights awaken as dreams fly.
Joyful whispers, tender light,
Painting magic through the night.

With laughter shared beneath the moon,
Every heart begins to bloom.
In the darkness, sparks ignite,
Joyful starlight, pure and bright.

Playful breezes dance with grace,
Chasing shadows, leaving trace.
In delight we sway and spin,
Together, let the magic begin.

Moments captured, softly spun,
In this realm, we all are one.
With every twinkle, every sigh,
Joyful starlight, you and I.

As dawn approaches, dreams remain,
Memories woven without a chain.
In playful realms where spirits soar,
Joyful starlight forevermore.

Traces of Happiness in Sunlit Fantasies

In the warmth of morning's kiss,
Sunlit dreams bring gentle bliss.
Happiness blooms in every glance,
In this light, our spirits dance.

With vibrant colors, joy unfolds,
Stories told, both new and old.
In the garden where hopes ignite,
Traces of laughter take their flight.

Whispers of love weave through the trees,
Carried softly on the breeze.
In every petal, echoes stay,
Sunlit fantasies lead the way.

As shadows fade and sunlight gleams,
We gather all our brightest dreams.
In this realm, our hearts align,
In sunlit glories, we entwine.

With grateful hearts, we chase the skies,
In happiness, our spirit flies.
Traces linger, sweet and free,
In sunlit fantasies, you and me.

Starlit Murmurs of Happiness

Beneath the starry, twinkling skies,
Whispers of joy in soft replies.
Moonlight dances on laughter's tune,
Chasing shadows, we're over the moon.

Each twinkle tells a tale untold,
Of dreams woven with threads of gold.
In this night, our spirits soar,
We find the happiness we adore.

Gentle breezes carry our sighs,
Echoes of love, as time gently flies.
In the silence, hearts sing bright,
Murmurs of bliss under the night.

Stars align in a cosmic embrace,
Revealing joy in our shared space.
With every wish on wings we send,
Starlit promise, joy will never end.

In laughter's grace, we find our way,
Each moment cherished, come what may.
Together we dance, twinkle, and shine,
In this starlit world, you are mine.

The Soft Embrace of Radiance

In dawn's first light, soft and warm,
A gentle glow begins to charm.
The world awakens from its sleep,
In radiance, our vows we keep.

When shadows fade, the colors blaze,
Painting moments in vibrant ways.
With every brush, love's touch unfolds,
In soft embraces, our hearts behold.

Golden rays dance across the floor,
Opening paths to dream and explore.
In this glow, we find our place,
Unraveling time in a tender space.

Nature sings with every hue,
The soft embrace of me and you.
Wrapped in warmth, together we stand,
As sunlight spills across the land.

In twilight's reach, our shadows blend,
A radiant glow, love's perfect end.
As stars ignite in evening's grace,
We bask in joy's warm embrace.

Laughter Beneath Celestial Canopies

Underneath a sky so wide,
We share our dreams with hearts open wide.
Every chuckle, a star takes flight,
Laughter echoes through the night.

Beneath celestial canopies bright,
We find our rhythm in pure delight.
With every giggle, our spirits rise,
Painting joy across the skies.

The constellations wink and sway,
In night's embrace, we dance and play.
Each sound a song, a sweet refrain,
Laughter mingling like gentle rain.

In fields of dreams, we lay side by side,
Bathed in moonlight, our laughter's guide.
With every moment, we build our dreams,
Underneath these celestial beams.

Through galaxies of unspoken bliss,
We seal our joys with a tender kiss.
In this laughter, our hearts are free,
Beneath the stars, just you and me.

Twilight's Serenade of Joyful Dreams

As twilight falls, a song takes flight,
Filling hearts with pure delight.
Each note a whisper, soft and low,
Of joyful dreams that gently flow.

The sky ablaze with hues so bright,
Guides us through the peaceful night.
In this serenade, our spirits soar,
Awakening hopes we can't ignore.

Shadows dance in the fading light,
Dreams awaken with the velvet night.
Every star sings a lullaby clear,
Wrapped in magic, love draws near.

In twilight's arms, we share a glance,
Lost in the beauty of this romance.
With every heartbeat, dreams align,
In this serenade, forever mine.

Together we weave a tapestry bright,
Of shimmering dreams that twinkle at night.
In twilight's embrace, we find our way,
Joyful dreams guiding night and day.

The Spark of Candor in the Golden Hour

In twilight's glow, the truth is clear,
Words spoken softly, drawing near.
With every glance, sincerity shines,
A moment captured, where love aligns.

The golden light, it paints our skin,
Whispers of honesty, where hearts begin.
In this embrace, we find our grace,
Time stands still, in this sacred space.

Candor ignites the path we tread,
In the soft hour, all doubts shed.
With laughter shared and stories spun,
Together in truth, we are one.

Each secret spoken, a gentle gift,
An honest heart, the perfect lift.
In the fading sun, we find our way,
The spark of candor lights the day.

Cheerful Echoes and Warm Embraces

In laughter's joy, we come alive,
With cheerful echoes, we thrive.
Warm embraces, a gentle bind,
In every hug, sweet love we find.

The whispers soft in evening light,
A world of warmth, holding tight.
Each joyful shout, a melody sweet,
Our hearts entwined, the perfect beat.

Through ups and downs, we dance along,
In every moment, we belong.
With open arms, we greet the day,
In cheerful echoes, we find our way.

The laughter shared, a radiant spark,
In the quiet hours, love leaves its mark.
Together, we weave a vibrant dream,
In warm embraces, life's a gleam.

Within this space, where love cascades,
We find our strength, as joy invades.
With every cheer that fills the air,
In echoes bright, our hearts lay bare.

Subtle Glimmers of Endearing Humor

In fleeting moments, laughter sways,
Subtle glimmers in bright arrays.
A wink shared here, a smile exchanged,
In simple jest, our hearts are ranged.

With playful tales that twist and bend,
The humor springs, a joyful blend.
With every laugh, the worries fade,
In endearing quirks, our bonds are made.

A gentle tease, a light embrace,
In silly antics, we find our place.
The joy of living, a playful tune,
In the laughter shared, we find our boon.

As stars align in evening's glow,
With every chuckle, our spirits flow.
In shared delight, we find our way,
Subtle glimmers light the day.

Together we dance in joy's sweet sway,
In humor's embrace, we laugh and play.
Each endearing moment, a treasured spark,
In glimmers of light, we leave our mark.

Shimmering Memories and Joyful Whimsy

In sparkling dreams, the past unfolds,
Shimmering memories, a tale retold.
Joyful whimsy paints the sky,
In every laugh, we lift and fly.

The echo of joy in every glance,
In childhood echoes, we take a chance.
With wishes whispered on gentle nights,
In shimmering moments, our hearts take flight.

The playful winds carry our songs,
In joy's embrace, where we belong.
With innocent glints in sparkling eyes,
We chase the dreams that never die.

In shared adventures, we find delight,
Together we spark the very night.
With whimsy weaving through all we do,
Shimmering moments, so bright and true.

For every memory, a story we write,
In joyful hearts, we dance in light.
With laughter ringing in every space,
In shimmering dreams, we find our place.